DISCARD

WATER ENERGY

GRAHAM RICKARD

Gareth Stevens Children's Books
MILWAUKEE

Titles in the Alternative Energy series:

Bioenergy
Geothermal Energy
Solar Energy
Water Energy
Wind Energy

For a free color catalog describing Gareth Stevens' list of high-quality children's books, call 1-800-341-3569 (USA) or 1-800-461-9120 (Canada).

Library of Congress Cataloging-in-Publication Data

Rickard, Graham.
    Water energy / Graham Rickard.
      p. cm. — (Alternative energy)
    "First published in the United Kingdom, copyright 1990, by Wayland
(Publishers) Limited"—T.p. verso.
    Includes index.
    Summary: Describes the resurgence of water power, one of the oldest
forms of alternative energy, and ways of using water as energy.
    ISBN 0-8368-0710-3
    1. Hydroelectric power plants—Juvenile literature. 2. Water-power—
Juvenile literature. [1. Hydroelectric power plants. 2. Water power.] I. Title.
II. Series: Alternative energy (Milwaukee, Wis.)
TK1081.R53   1991
620.1'06—dc20   91-9260

17.95   *E.1 C.1*

North American edition first published in 1991 by

Gareth Stevens Children's Books
1555 North RiverCenter Drive, Suite 201
Milwaukee, Wisconsin 53212, USA

Picture acknowledgements

Artwork by Nick Hawken

The publishers would like to thank the following for supplying photographs: J. Allan Cash Picture Library, 4 (left),
5, 6, 7 (upper), 26; Bruce Coleman, 8; Energy Technology Support Unit, 12, 16, 24 (right); Environmental Picture
Library, 17 (upper); Geoscience Features Picture Library, 4 (right); Robert Harding Picture Library, cover;
National Power, 11; Oxford Scientific Films, 7 (lower); Photri, 18; Science Photo Library, 24 (left); Snowy
Mountains Hydro-Electric Authority, 22 (right), 25; Tony Stone, 23; Tasmanian Hydro-Electric Commission, 9;
Topham Picture Library, 17 (lower); U.S. Department of Energy, 22 (left); Zefa Picture Library, 14.

Editors (U.K.): Paul Mason and William Wharfe
Editors (U.S.): Eileen Foran and John D. Rateliff
Designer: Charles Harford

Printed in Italy

1 2 3 4 5 6 7 8 9 95 94 93 92 91

Contents

Words that appear in the glossary are printed in **boldface** type the first time they appear in the text.

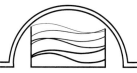

WHY ALTERNATIVE ENERGY?

Energy is the ability to do work. All animals and plants need energy in order to live. All machines need energy to make them work. As the world's population increases and people use more machines, more energy is needed to power them. The world's demand for energy has increased by more than ten times since the beginning of this century.

Most of this energy is produced by burning one of three **fossil fuels** — oil, natural gas, and coal. But there is only so much fossil fuel in the world. Supplies that took millions of years to build up are being burned at the rate of over half a million tons an hour. At this rate, all the world's oil and gas will be gone by the year 2040.

Cleaning up an oil slick at sea.

Coal-fired power stations caused the acid rain that killed these trees.

Coal-fired power stations release large amounts of pollution into the atmosphere. This causes acid rain, which kills trees and pollutes lakes. Here we see the chimneys of a coal-fired power station in Romania.

Even worse, fossil fuels cause serious damage to the environment. When they burn, fossil fuels produce poisonous gases that turn into **acid rain**. Acid rain pollutes vast areas of the world, killing trees, fish, and wildlife. These gases also contribute to the **greenhouse effect**, which is gradually warming up the Earth's atmosphere.

Because of all these problems, people all over the world are looking for alternative sources of energy. Some people see the use of **nuclear energy** as the best alternative to fossil fuels.

But nuclear energy depends on supplies of uranium, which is even rarer than the fossil fuels we use now. Also, the pollution caused by nuclear energy is far more dangerous than anything produced by fossil fuels. So scientists and environmentalists are working together to come up with safe, clean, and renewable sources of energy.

This book looks at the different ways of using water energy as an alternative energy source. Water energy is renewable, and, unlike coal, natural gas, or oil, it will not run out.

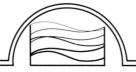

THE POWER OF WATER

Four-fifths of the world is covered by water. The water in our oceans and rivers is constantly on the move. Waves, currents, tides, flowing rivers, and waterfalls all contain vast amounts of **kinetic energy**, the energy found in all moving things. Water can be used as a source of energy by converting its kinetic energy into electricity. Increased use of water energy could reduce our need to use fossil fuels.

Water is one of our oldest energy sources. The water wheel was probably first used in Greece, in the first century B.C. By the Middle Ages, water wheels were used throughout Europe and Asia for grinding grain in mills, powering bellows in forges, and

This view from space shows just how much of the Earth's surface is covered by water. Here we see both the Pacific Ocean (left) and the Atlantic Ocean (right).

irrigating fields. Almost every village had its own mill, run entirely by waterpower.

Above: The water of Niagara Falls, on the border between the United States and Canada, drops 164 feet (50 m) and has huge amounts of kinetic energy.

Right: A stream provides the power for this old mill in Virginia. The mill is used for grinding wheat for bread.

This industrial water wheel powers a hammer that shapes metal.

The water wheel was the original power source of the **Industrial Revolution**, powering the machinery of the first factories.

These factories were usually built alongside rivers to make sure that there would be a constant source of power. Eventually, the invention of steam engines, which could power bigger machines than could water wheels, meant that water wheels were no longer used.

In Britain alone, there are 20,000 abandoned sites where water wheels were once used. Today, almost all this waterpower remains unused.

Hydroelectric power plants have so far proved the most successful way of harnessing water energy. These power plants use moving water from rivers or reservoirs to turn the **turbines** that power electric **generators**.

The seas and oceans of the world are also good energy sources. Some plans, already in operation, depend on tides to generate electricity. Some experiments have attempted to capture the power of the waves, but so far, this is proving much more difficult and costly than other forms of water energy.

The use of any form of energy has its drawbacks. Although generating electricity from water energy produces little pollution, building hydroelectric dams means flooding vast areas of land.

Also, the barriers used in tidal power stations can change the environment along the seashore, affecting the natural **habitat** of many plants, birds, and other animals.

The Gordon Dam in Tasmania. Dams like this collect huge amounts of water that can be used to run hydroelectric power stations (see pages 20-21).

ENERGY FROM THE TIDES

Every day, the gravity of both the Sun and the Moon pulls on the Earth and moves vast quantities of water in the world's seas. We call these movements **tides**.

Tidal power was first harnessed by tidal mills (water wheels powered by incoming or outgoing tides) around 1,000 years ago. At high tide, water was trapped behind a **floodgate**. As the tide went out, the floodgate was opened to power a water wheel.

Modern tidal power stations work the same way. They capture the water behind a **barrage**, or wall, at high tide. At low tide, the water is released through turbines to produce electricity.

The gravity of the Sun and the Moon causes tides.

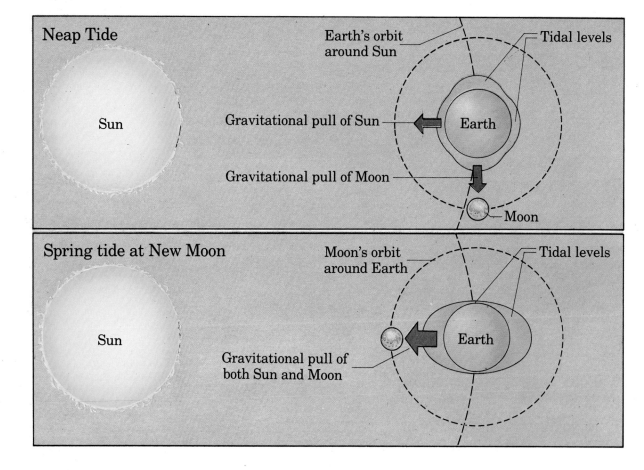

The barrage over the Rance River, seen as the tide goes out.

Tidal power stations are already in use in Canada, France, the Soviet Union, and China. The best-known one is on the **estuary** of the Rance River, in northern France. The tide here rises and falls 44 feet (13.4 m). The power station consists of a single barrage across the estuary. This contains 24 turbines attached to generators that produce 320 **megawatts (MW)** of electricity — enough to boil about 150,000 kettles. The barrage is a long, straight dam with a road on top, so it acts as a bridge as well as a power station. The turbines work in two directions, both when the water flows into the estuary as the tide comes in, and when the tide goes out.

Tidal power stations work best where there is a large estuary and a big difference between how high the water gets at high tide and low tide. A possible site for a tidal barrage is the Bay of Fundy, between New Brunswick and

An artist's impression of the proposed Severn barrage.

Nova Scotia. A tidal power station here would generate as much electricity as a power station run by fossil fuels, without the pollution caused by burning oil or coal.

Several sites around Britain are ideally suited to use tidal energy. Tidal barrages could produce as much as 8 percent of that country's energy needs. One of the best sites is the Severn estuary, where high tide is 36 feet (11 m) higher than low tide. The proposed Severn barrage would be 11 miles (18 km) long and would contain 216 turbines, with floodgates to control the flow of water on either side. Enormous **locks** at one end would allow ships to pass through the barrage. The amount of electricity produced would be about 8 billion watts.

Tidal barrages are expensive and difficult to build. When they are completed, however, they produce cheap electricity, use no fuel, and are easy to run and maintain. A major problem with tidal power stations, though, is that they do not always produce power when it is most needed. This is because the times of high and low tides are constantly changing.

Tidal power stations have their own environmental problems. Salmon, eels, and other migrating fish that swim up estuaries and rivers to breed are killed when they pass through the turbines. The barrage creates a large, shallow pool behind it that floods mud flats and marshes, destroying the homes of many birds and other wildlife, some of them already endangered species.

At the same time, the artificial salt lake created by building the barrage is often an ideal spot for water sports, encouraging the growth of tourism.

Opposite: How a tidal barrage works.

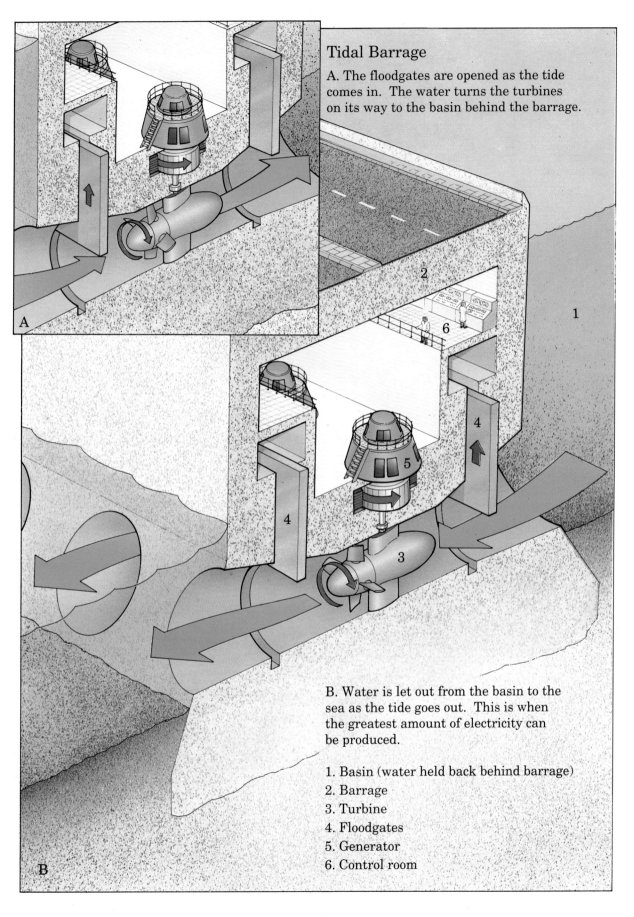

Tidal Barrage

A. The floodgates are opened as the tide comes in. The water turns the turbines on its way to the basin behind the barrage.

B. Water is let out from the basin to the sea as the tide goes out. This is when the greatest amount of electricity can be produced.

1. Basin (water held back behind barrage)
2. Barrage
3. Turbine
4. Floodgates
5. Generator
6. Control room

POWER FROM WAVES

Every day, the world's coasts are battered by waves of enormous power. Ocean waves are created by winds blowing over the sea. Scientists have been looking for ways to turn the constant rising and falling of waves into useful energy.

In some places, waves can be up to 82 feet (25 m) high. It is estimated that the energy in only one yard (0.9 m) of the biggest

Waves contain large amounts of kinetic energy.

waves along some coasts could generate 100 **kilowatts (kW)** of power. Even if only a third of this power is converted into electricity, wave power stations could become important sources of energy.

Over 300 designs for wave-energy converters already exist. In some designs, the up-and-down movement of a device floating in the water is used to pump fluid to turbines that drive a generator. The Salter Duck design consists of twenty to thirty "ducks," or floats. The bobbing motion of the ducks drives a pump. The pump turns a turbine, which drives a generator. The Salter Duck uses most of the wave's energy.

One of the most successful designs uses the **oscillating** water column (OWC) principle. A box with an underwater opening contains a column of water, which acts like a piston in a cylinder. As the water column moves up and down with the waves, air is forced in and out through a turbine at the top. This drives a generator.

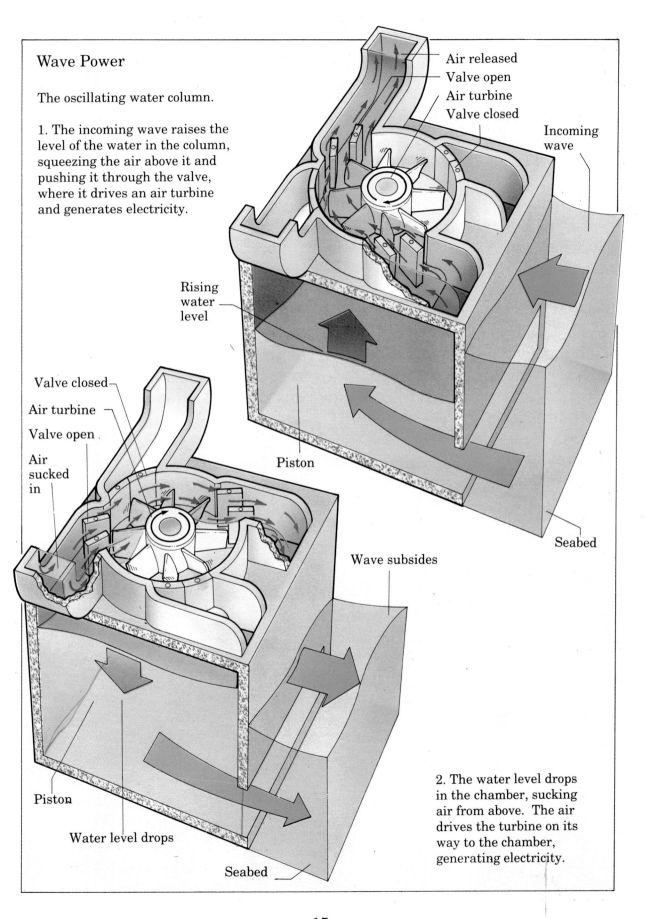

Wave Power

The oscillating water column.

1. The incoming wave raises the level of the water in the column, squeezing the air above it and pushing it through the valve, where it drives an air turbine and generates electricity.

Air released

Valve open

Air turbine

Valve closed

Incoming wave

Rising water level

Piston

Seabed

Valve closed

Air turbine

Valve open

Air sucked in

Wave subsides

Piston

Water level drops

Seabed

2. The water level drops in the chamber, sucking air from above. The air drives the turbine on its way to the chamber, generating electricity.

The first successful OWC device was used in Japan to power a light on a navigation **buoy**. Another OWC device has been installed on a cliff at Tofteshallen, Norway. One of the most advanced wave-energy devices in the world, it can generate 500 kW of power.

Wave-energy devices are difficult to build because they must be strong enough to withstand battering from wind and waves, and some designs have to be light enough to float. It is also important to be able to store some of the electricity produced when the sea is rough, so that power can be provided even when the sea is calm.

Wave-energy power stations are expensive to build and are difficult to anchor. They also pose a danger to shipping and interfere with the wave pattern on nearby shores. In some places, wave-energy power stations may speed the process of erosion, which could, in turn, affect beaches and wildlife.

This is an artist's impression of a large-scale wave-power scheme, with rows of wave-power machines.

One way around this is for scientists to develop small wave-energy devices. These would be useful in providing power for small, isolated coastal communities, which now depend on expensive diesel fuel to generate electricity.

Right: The wave-power machine built on the cliffs at Tofteshallen, Norway. In 1989, this wave-power machine was damaged during a fierce storm. Future devices will have to be stronger.

Below: Wave-power machines must be designed to stand up to the destructive force of the rough sea.

HEAT FROM THE SEA

In hot climates, the sea absorbs vast amounts of the Sun's heat. This heat can be converted into electricity. The idea of using heat from the sea was first thought of over 100 years ago. However, it was not until the 1920s that the first electricity-generating process was devised. The process is called ocean thermal energy conversion (OTEC).

In tropical regions, the upper, Sun-heated seawater is much warmer than the deeper water. At the equator, for example, the temperature changes from 79°F (26°C) at the surface to about 40°F (4.4°C) at a depth of 2,500 feet (760 m). The OTEC unit uses warm water from the upper layer to **evaporate** a liquid that boils at a very low temperature, such as ammonia or Freon. The gas produced by the evaporation is used as steam is used in a conventional power station.

Opposite: A proposed OTEC design.

Below: In tropical regions, the Sun warms the sea. This warmth can be used to produce electricity.

1. Helicopter pad
2. Crew living quarters
3. Warm-surface-water inlet
4. Ammonia or Freon storage tank
5. Ballast tanks
6. Evaporator
7. Turbines
8. Control room
9. Generator
10. Condenser
11. Buoyancy tanks
12. Cold-water inlet, about 230 feet (70 m) under the surface
13. Cables transmitting electricity to mainland
14. Cold-water outlet
15. Warm-water outlet

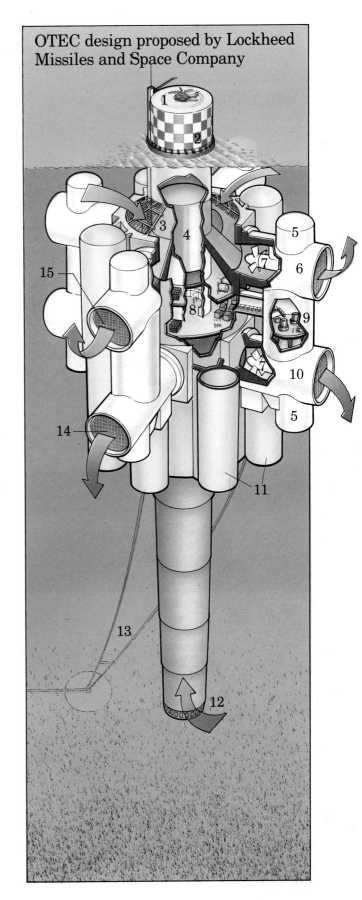

OTEC design proposed by Lockheed Missiles and Space Company

The gas is used to turn a turbine, which drives a generator to produce electricity. The gas is then turned back into liquid by cooling it with cold water drawn up from the bottom of the sea. The liquid ammonia or Freon is then pumped back to the evaporator and used again.

Only small-scale experiments with OTEC units have been carried out so far. The largest OTEC generator is a 100-kW plant in Japan. Another, in operation in the Pacific Ocean, near Hawaii, generates 50 kW. If these tests prove successful, bigger OTEC units may be built, probably designed to produce 2 MW — enough electricity for 1,000 homes.

How hydroelectric plants work.

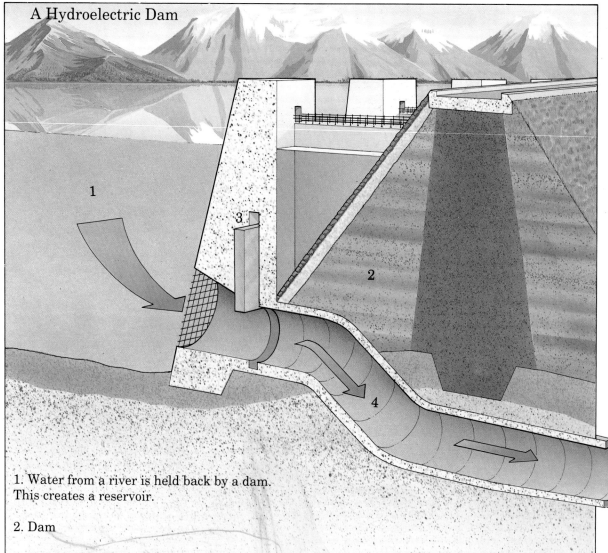

A Hydroelectric Dam

1. Water from a river is held back by a dam.
This creates a reservoir.

2. Dam

3. Floodgate — this can be raised or lowered
to control the flow of water

4. Water flows down through tunnel,
gathering speed

5. Tunnel gets narrower — this increases
the speed of the water going through
the turbine

6. Turbine is spun around by the water

7. Dynamo inside generator spins,
generating electricity

8. Control room

9. Water flows out of the turbine back
to the river

HYDROELECTRIC POWER

Falling water is probably the world's largest renewable energy source. The Sun evaporates water from the Earth's surface. The water then falls as rain or snow over hills and mountains and flows back down to the sea. Hydroelectric plants use the kinetic energy of falling water, either in a natural river or from a **reservoir** created by an artificial dam. This water is fed through

tunnels to turn turbines, which drive electric generators.

The amount of electricity that these generators can produce depends on how much water is flowing and how far the water falls as it goes through the turbines.

Below: Inside a hydroelectric dam.

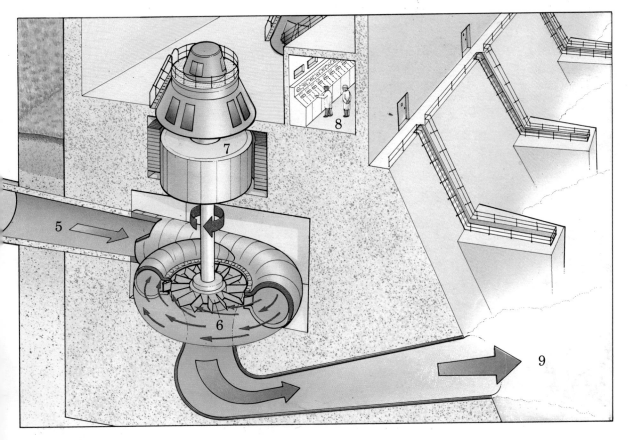

The Grand Coulee Dam, the largest concrete structure in the world.

An inside view of a hydroelectric station, showing the tops of the generators.

A small amount of water falling from a great height can produce as much power as a large amount of water falling a shorter distance. This means a small dam high up in the mountains can produce as much power as a large dam near the same river's mouth.

In some ways, hydroelectric power is a cheap source of energy. However, it is very expensive to build a dam and power station. For instance, imagine how much it would cost to build a concrete wall 550 feet (168 m) tall! Yet that's the height of the Grand Coulee Dam in Washington State, which supplies electricity to thousands of people in the northwestern United States.

Once a hydroelectric dam is in place, the cost of producing electricity is small. Water is free, and a large power plant can be run by only a few people. No fuel is needed to run this type of dam, and the same river can be dammed at several different places as it flows downhill, using the same water to produce even more power. However, many countries can't afford to dam their rivers because it is expensive to do so. The United States, the Soviet Union, Britain, and China have all helped developing countries build hydroelectric dams.

Hydroelectric dams can also cause environmental problems. Huge dams raise the water level behind them, flooding enormous areas of land. Whenever water is diverted from one area to another, it can badly hurt the plants and wildlife that live in both areas. It can also have useful effects. For instance, in Egypt and Australia, irrigation dams have helped turn previously dry desert regions into rich, green farmland.

Hydroelectric power plants can also be used to store energy. In the early hours of the day, when people are asleep, there is a very low demand for electricity. Conventional power stations cannot just "switch off," however. They keep generating electricity even when no one is there to use it, so a lot of energy goes to waste.

Dams can provide water to irrigate farmland that would otherwise be dry.

Inside the "Electric Mountain" at Dinorwic, Wales.

A small-scale hydroelectric turbine.

One way that hydroelectric plants can avoid this waste is to use the surplus electricity to pump water into a second reservoir. When an extra supply of power is needed, the water can fall back into the main reservoir behind the dam. As the water falls, it powers the turbines.

A system of this type was built at Dinorwic, Wales. It is called the "Electric Mountain" because between the reservoirs, the water falls through tunnels that are hollowed out of a mountain. Dinorwic produces enough electricity to light up a city.

Large-scale hydroelectric plants already produce 6.7 percent of the world's total energy needs — twice as much as the nuclear power industry's share.

There is now evidence that water wheels and small-scale hydro-electric plants could be very useful for small towns in remote places. They could provide cheap electricity for towns that presently rely on generators powered by expensive diesel fuel. Scientists have improved designs of small-scale turbines and generators so much that the devices can work even in fairly shallow rivers.

The Snowy Mountains system

One of the best examples of large-scale hydroelectric power in action is in the Snowy Mountains of Australia. Australia is the driest and flattest of all the continents. Half the land receives less than 12 inches (30 cm) of rain a year, and most of the rest of the country receives less than 24 inches (61 cm). Australia's largest river, the Murray, takes a whole year to empty into the sea as much water as South America's largest river, the Amazon, does in one-and-a-half days. The only area in Australia where there is a lot of water is the mountainous Great Dividing Range.

The Great Dividing Range stretches north to south along the eastern edge of the country. Winds from the sea drop their moisture as they cross these mountains. This rain and snow forms many streams and rivers. At the southern end, the mountain range rises to about 6,900 feet (2,100 m) above sea level and is called the Snowy Mountains.

Construction on the Snowy Mountains hydroelectric system in the 1950s.

After World War II, Australia had to produce more energy to supply its rapidly growing industry. Also, more water was needed for crops. Several ideas were put forward to use the waters of the Snowy River for electrical power and for irrigation. One of these plans, the Snowy Mountains Scheme, diverts the waters of the Snowy and the Eucumbene rivers through two massive systems of tunnels. These feed the Murray and Murrumbidgee rivers with extra water for irrigation. The water falls 2,600 feet (790 m) through tunnels, shafts, and power stations to generate electricity.

The Snowy River Scheme took 25 years to build. It is the largest hydroelectric system in the world, covering an area of over 1,235 square miles (3,200 sq km) and costing about $750 million to build. It includes 16 large dams, 7 power stations, over 90 miles (145 km) of tunnels, 50 miles (80 km) of **aqueducts**, a pumping station, and hundreds of miles of transmission lines. It is one of the largest engineering projects in Australia. It provides nearly 4 billion watts of electricity and huge quantities of water for irrigation.

From the simplest water wheels to huge projects like the Snowy Mountains system, waterpower today provides the world with clean, safe, and renewable energy. Waterpower will become even more important in meeting the energy challenges of the future.

Opposite: One section of the huge Snowy Mountains hydroelectric system.

Below: Water drops 1,475 feet (450 m) through pipes to the Murray 1 station.

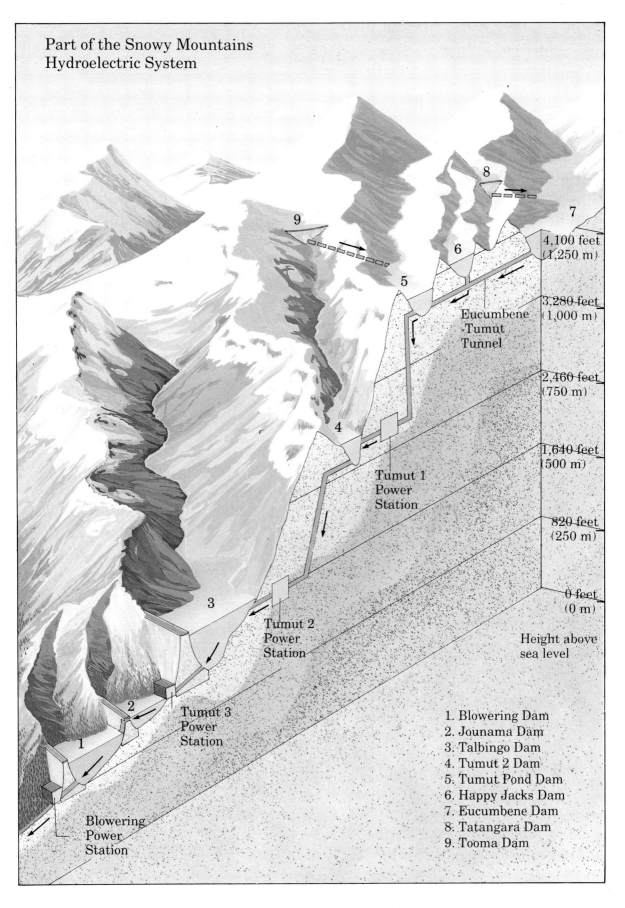

Part of the Snowy Mountains
Hydroelectric System

4,100 feet
(1,250 m)

3,280 feet
(1,000 m)

Eucumbene
-Tumut
Tunnel

2,460 feet
(750 m)

1,640 feet
(500 m)

Tumut 1
Power
Station

820 feet
(250 m)

0 feet
(0 m)

Height above
sea level

Tumut 2
Power
Station

Tumut 3
Power
Station

Blowering
Power
Station

1. Blowering Dam
2. Jounama Dam
3. Talbingo Dam
4. Tumut 2 Dam
5. Tumut Pond Dam
6. Happy Jacks Dam
7. Eucumbene Dam
8. Tatangara Dam
9. Tooma Dam

PROJECT

You will need:

- A 4.5-volt electric motor with a small gear attached

- A 1.5-volt light bulb in a socket

- A plastic soda bottle

- A cork

- Two squeeze tops from dishwashing-liquid bottles

- Wire from a coat hanger

- A large gear

- Nonsoluble glue

- Two wooden blocks

- The casing from a ballpoint pen

- Screws, a screwdriver, tape, and scissors

How to build your own water wheel:

1. Ask an adult to push the wire through the cork so that the wire sticks out slightly on one end.

2. Cut eight strips of plastic from a soda bottle. The strips should be the same length as the cork and one inch (2.5 cm) wide.

3. Ask an adult to cut grooves in the cork for you to stick the plastic strips into (see diagram).

4. Glue the plastic strips into the cork's grooves. They should stick out at least one inch (2.5 cm).

5. Slide the other end of the wire through the pen casing and the bottle tops (see diagram). Fix the large gear to the end of the wire.

6. Tape the pen casing to a wooden block. Place the block on the edge of a kitchen sink. The water wheel should be directly beneath the faucet. Tape the water wheel to the counter.

7. Screw the motor to the second block. Connect the motor's wires to the light bulb. The large and small gears should interlock.

8. Turn the faucet on gently, slowly increasing the flow until the water wheel begins to spin.

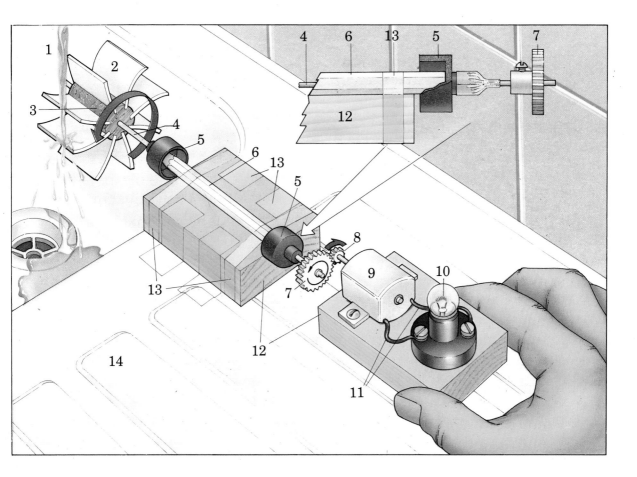

1. Water from faucet
2. Strips of plastic from a soda bottle
3. Cork
4. Wire from coat hanger
5. Squeeze tops from dishwashing-liquid bottles
6. Empty casing from a ballpoint pen
7. Large gear

8. Small gear
9. 4.5-volt motor
10. 1.5-volt light bulb
11. Electric wires
12. Wooden blocks
13. Tape
14. Counter top

Press the gears together firmly. The faster the gears turn, the more electricity you will generate.

Note:

The water wheel takes energy from the running water and uses it to turn the large gear. The large gear turns the small wheel attached to the motor.

The motor turns the energy into electricity and uses it to light the light bulb. See what happens when the water wheel goes faster and then slower.

Glossary

Acid rain: Rain formed by pollution in the air combining with water vapor in clouds. It kills trees and wildlife and, in time, can even eat away stone.

Aqueduct: An artificial above-ground channel used for carrying water.

Barrage: A long, low barrier or dam built across an estuary.

Buoy: A floating marker that serves as a guide to ships.

Estuary: An inlet of the sea formed by the mouth of a wide river.

Evaporate: To change from a liquid into a gas.

Floodgates: Movable gates that, when closed, stop the flow of water through a barrage or dam.

Fossil fuels: Energy sources, such as coal, oil, and natural gas, formed from the remains of plants and animals that lived millions of years ago.

Generator: A machine that generates, or produces, electricity.

Greenhouse effect: The warming of the Earth due to gases in the atmosphere that trap the Sun's heat.

Habitat: A place where an animal or plant usually lives.

Hydroelectric: Producing electricity from falling water.

Industrial Revolution: The sudden change that took place in the late eighteenth century from handmade goods to machine-made, mass-produced items made in factories.

Irrigating: Supplying with water by means of a system of ditches, pipes, or canals.

Kilowatt (kW): A thousand watts (see **Watt**).

Kinetic energy: The energy contained in all moving objects.

Lock: A section of a river or canal set off by floodgates. It is used to enable ships to get from one water level to another.

Megawatt (MW): A million watts (see **Watt**).

Nuclear energy: Energy produced by splitting or combining atoms.

Oscillation: Any back-and-forth motion, whether from side to side or up and down.

Reservoir: A place where a large amount of water is collected and stored for use.

Turbine: A device, shaped somewhat like a propeller, which can spin to power electric generators.

Watt: A unit of electrical power. It takes 60 to 100 watts to power most light bulbs.

Books to Read

Dams. Cass R. Sandak (Franklin Watts)
Grand Coulee: A Story of the Columbia River from Molten Lavas and Ice to Grand Coulee Dam. Wallace Baljo, Jr. (Clipboard)
Small Energy Sources: Choices that Work. Augusta Goldin (Harcourt Brace Jovanovich)
Water. John Satchwell (Franklin Watts)
The Water Book: Where It Came from and Where It Goes. Ira M. Freeman and Sean Morrison (Random House)
Water, Water! Tom Johnston (Gareth Stevens)
Wind and Water Energy. Sherry Payne (Raintree)
Working with Water. Neil Ardley (Franklin Watts)

Places to Write

These groups can help you find out more about water energy and alternative energy in general. When you write, be sure to ask specific questions, and always include your full name, address, and age.

In the United States:

Conservation and Renewable Energy Inquiry and Referral Service
P.O. Box 8900
Silver Spring, MD 20907

International Water Resources Association
205 North Mathews Avenue
University of Illinois
Urbana, IL 61801

In Canada:

Efficiency and Alternative Energy Technology Board Department of Energy, Mines, and Resources
580 Booth Street, 7th Floor
Ottawa, Ontario K1A 0E4

Planetary Association for Clean Energy
100 Bronson Avenue, Suite 1001
Ottawa, Ontario K1R 6G8

Index

A **boldface** number means that the entry is illustrated on that page.